Elija's Mistake

Tales
from the
Serengeti

Elija was a
juvenile
elephant, who was
not too young
and not too old.
He admired the great
matriarch,
the elephant who led
the herd in a nice
STRAIGHT
line to safety,
food and water.

One day Elija watched the animals of the plains gathering for their migration, in a completely *disorganized fashion.* A sudden idea came to him, this was his **b i g** chance to become a **leader** too!

He marched
DOWN
and encouraged
the wildebeest
and zebras
to join him
on the trek to the
short **grass**
plains.

After Elija had

persuaded a

small

group of followers

to join him, they all

set out in a neat,

STRAIGHT LINE,

one behind the other

in an orderly fashion.

It was not
v e r y   l o n g,
however, before
the animals
tired
of walking one by one
and began pairing up
so they could talk
to each other
along the way.

Elija kept looking back
to check that his herd
remained in a
STRAIGHT LINE
and began to
scold
those who
walked out of formation.

As Elija trod on,
his line continued to
get worse and worse,
but he would
not give up.
He was now so
caught up
in maintaining
the line that...

He was constantly looking back and **hollering** orders, no longer **watching** their path at all.

PHOOMPH!

Elija suddenly found
his head, ears,
and most of his trunk,
stuck in the hollow of
an old baobab tree!

The animals
snorted and **laughed**
as Elija tried to get free.
They were tired of their
bossy
young leader and
so they each went
merrily on their way.

It was then that the **great matriarch** showed up and smiled as she helped Elija out of the tree. "That was a very good try, Elija," she gently said. "You're bound to succeed now that you know there is more to being a **leader** than being first in line."